HYBRID HEAVEN
& other(ed) poems

By the same author:

Poetry:

Japanabandon
Manifest.oh!
Diaspora^3
Objections, Scars & Artefacts
Outside of Here. Outsider Hear!
Childish Recollections (forthcoming)

Other works:

Nicked Names (novella)

HYBRID HEAVEN
& other(ed) poems

ANDREW GEOFFREY KWABENA MOSS

Hybrid Heaven & other(ed) poems
Recent Work Press
Canberra, Australia

ISBN: 9781764106894 (paperback)

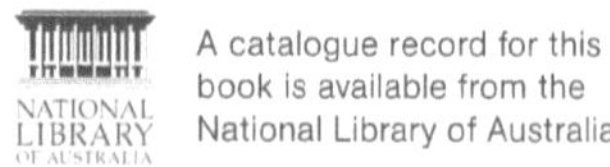

Cover image: The Adinkra symbol *Funtumfunefu Denkyemfunefu*
Set by Recent Work Press

recentworkpress.com

SS

To Mum, Dad & Mike,
and the Anglo-Ghanaian
materials in 84 Regent Street

Note on the Cover

The Adinkra symbol *Funtumfunefu Denkyemfunefu* depicts two crocodiles sharing a single stomach. It represents unity in diversity: distinct identities bound by a common destiny.

Derived from the proverb:

Funtumfunafu Denkyemfunafu, wowo yafunu koro nanso wonya biribi a wofom efiri se aduane no de no yete no wo menetwitwie mu—

They share one stomach, yet struggle over food, for its sweetness is felt as it passes through the throat.

Contents

At the Polo

Onto the modernist flat, trapezoid prism roof,
A white eagle swoops
The godlo's wings splay Turner
& O'Connor neighbourhoods
Its crowned talons & regal beak
reach Mount Kosciuszko,
down the Snowy Hydro
via Namadgi & Black Mountain poles
apart yet united red shield

At the Polo, heavy rimmed glasses
magnify the shoeshine's funereal overcoat
The white-haired face asks if we're customers
He nods us on in husky overtones

Witamy chalks a crowded blackboard,
in a flourish of bubble calligraphy,
stuffed with pierogi,
dumplings & golabki cabbage rolls
for Jew & Gentile Pokies free socials
For Pole & non-Pole

Opposite, students wrap up in the loop
of Dr. Who scarves,
time travellers from a seventies TARDIS,
Eco warriors in hiking boots & Nepalese fleeces,
chunky translucent step sepia soles
Doc Marten loafers juxtapose
with the French Resistance
white pop socks, once more Top of the Pops

***

Zapraszamy! An invitation to Old Country blues
under the Cardinal Wojtyla's crayoned eyes
A silver bell tinkles service with a smile
for forest foragers

Soplica viscous honey drips from the tap
Pigwowa liquor sits above the aspic fridge
unchastised vodka belt nations
buckle under the weight of temptation
Patrons neck shots, in glass trinkets
Sto lat in spirit levelled meniscus ring

We consider which vodka to imbibe
Cherry or hazelnut Lipowa to Cracow
& silently debate Pigwowa's digraph
A pre-Google apricot or a quince mystery
The search engine provides appetite
to an aperitif surprise

We're joined by a boy whose earring dangles low
he solicits, 'Not a beer. Something Polish'
The barman's loose spiral stands attentively,
his furrowed brow & eyebrows sharply meet
A hybrid Uncle Fester & Frankenstein
proffers cucumber vodka, 'You'll be f-ine.'
We laugh at the sound of 'You'll be flying.'

***

The manager gives us a Copernicus tour
in whirlwind, he orbits Taglietti's 70s shrine
Astronomical polymaths illuminate

each dusty room narrates in fixed free verse
Andrew recalls at the ANU bar, Nirvana,
the ablution ratios of male to female loos
We digress to mutual friends
In this leafy corner of the inner west
Mary's mum, no less the Emeritus
Professor devised NSM
to rival Chomsky's generative grammar
as we tipple & lick viscous linguistic lips

Backstage, we enter a loft space
chipboard green rooms sharpie obscenities
on plywood, pre-performance sinks
bulbs around mirrors for sad clowns,
Bert Williams dancing in the dark,
daubed with cork mask
We look across gabled frames
where marionettes pull showbiz strings

Bar headed, we pass roosters
embroidered in folk art finery,
flora rosella bright
the cross-stitch of old history
Floral skirts burst & bloom into costumes
aprons germinate a spring instep, lace boots,
red rosaries bleed the coral necklaces
spinsters wreathed with ribbons

The deflowered don white kerchiefs on heads
& dance the *Mazur, Krakowiak,*
Polonez & Oberek
Men in peacock blue shake tailfeather tassels

dandies dressed in striped pants
grab quills from krakuska caps
All strutting in geometric appeal

***

At night's end, the white eagle retreats
wings, red shield, crown, golden beak
Its talons retract myths,
legends of birds, gods & monsters,
winged hussars on saddleback
For the hangover of misty dreams

Gilded armour glints
in the forest darkening
Wojtek, a bear & soldiers dance
as troops advance
to shift bordering thoughts
On Europe's auction a Soviet bloc anvil & gavel
caught under a new sickle & hammer
The bridge between east and west bows
As lasting orders call

Black Gypsies

for Sam Lambert & Shaka Maidoh

I met these tailors, DJing
mahogany tattooed arms blue back
on metallic bevel edged turntables

plated with heavy metal rings
Signets mixing history,
slapping cross faders

I met these tailors back & forth a Black Atlantic
behind the barricades from space
Invaders wearing ACF red

armbands part anarchy,
part swastika swami
Vodun gods laying syncretic needles

I met these tailors, for the record scratching heads
turning tables, pressing new studio labels
Shaka & Sam, new age travellers

without passports
beyond borders, beyond paranormal
invisible biometrics, joining dots of diaspora

I met these tailors, shapeshifters wearing trilbies
with biker jackets, gang bandanas,
black leather & neckerchiefs

preppy freshmen
carrying Varsity credential letters
in briefcases with urgency

I met these tailors, revising revisionist history
Black Gypsies dispersed like oware seeds
on the streets of Stockholm, Lisbon,

Afropeans in Marseille,
Berlin, Amsterdam, Hoxton, Calais
mixing with fashionable industry

I met these tailors stitching fables,
rude boy mods in parkas,
scooter horns for Brazzaville Billism

Stetsons on & bolos ties,
clinging to hip life jazz
suede jackets dangling tassels hypnotically

I met these tailors, in the Bad Brains club
forging ahead with heavy metal work,
Hendrix psychedelics & moodful mindful jazz

Lapel pins on & badges to honour
I met these tailors, at Anansi's loom
printing vintage Japanese denim
wearing gas masks & balaclavas
holding muzzled dogs in riot costume
to mix flavours from every lost continent,
they forage in ponchos to keep them warm
A bricolage past sticks with invisible pins

like Voodoo priests, seamlessly connecting
I met these tailors, punks rocksteady
in their ska, reggae, soul & heavy metal
turning tables, mixing history's beats

New age creatives, blackpacker
Afropeans, roaming the flea markets
Ghana's Makola to Togo's Lomé,
I met these tailors, treading the catwalks
like Jerry from Tom, thieves from police
In Paris, Tokyo, New York & Rome

Speeches in lace less brogues, homeless
mendicant mending fabrication
Barbed words wire defences, yet
they step out of the oversized trench coats
I met these tailors, flying past our world's war
missiles for an afrofuture seeking its heat
Afronauts at the cipher prophesize
like the Dogon, visited from Sirius B

Sewing their own labels,
sta-pressed to lapels like rare grooves
on green sleeves, envies for rewriting history
on dubplates, for turning monochrome
to techno-coloured dream sequined sequences
I met these tailors, in collaboration with Fred
Perry, laurels for these hardy laureates
Rudeboy skankin' piped down arms
in black & white icing, a magpie pecks worms
deep in vintage clothes piles, blacksmiths
at anvils hammering a message home

Mad hatters on a mercurial rise
Listening to two sevens clash with Jimmy Jazz
Black Panthers pouncing podiums
on the prowl, whiskers erect for messages
buried in the concrete jungle treasure, their project
extends from the Bronx to Brixton to Brazzaville
I met these tailors, in the ghetto next to Malcolm X
camouflaged in Lumumba & Mobutu leopard hats

Avec Ces Frères, Art Comes First
New traditions for modern nomads, the swagger
of Parisian savoir faire, Mayfair refinement
& borderless practicality, travelling tailoring
by travelling tailors made in the same cloth,
maps cartographers chart, as William Cuffay
his grandfather a slave from Ghana to St Kitts
I met these tailors, on an epic journey: UK to Australia

Cocky

Ice white splinters cut the grass
                                        into glass shards
Cocky flocks litter Spring baize
          On Eastgrove playing fields
   Gundungurra elders tell
   Of erasure

Billism

In Léopoldville ride the Bills
Cowboy hats, bolo ties & boots lasso
African & European neighbourhoods
Spurred on to scalp feather headed movies
in Kinshasa kerchiefs, jeans & shirts, worn by
Texas Bills facing Godzilla & King Kong
playing Cowboys & Indians

Canberra New & Old

At the Old Canberra Inn
a sparkling peacock cobalt shim
wiggles their tail feather no longer boa constricted
& enters over the rainbow bridge to new traditions
Dame Edna glasses uplift heavy mascara
the drag of a cigarette held between rouge lips
Engendered fluidities hiss out of the taps

An ABC journalist takes in florid IPA notes
Casting a glance for his date like discarded votes
Next Gen sauna buddies from Calabria
exchange Snowy Hydro scheme anecdotes
Macedonians, Greeks & Serbo-Croats
sit under rustic beams with glowing amber nectar
Fingers protect pints in honeycomb hourglass

Beads laced by CAPITAL Trail Pale Ale
Orange flames blaze magnified
Peter's cadence changes from South Australian
Port Pirie across the Nullarbor Plain
To dairy & Goulburn Valley irrigation
to a Godfather, hand pecking the air
Fingertips stick momentarily to bellissima lips

He recalls his Italian connection
Elbow deep pulling up spuds like stumps in Bayles
Pinching the screen of his iPhone, Vincenzo
showboats his renovated Kaleen home
Held up by Milanese pencil pines

The new façade of the Old
A rendered castle without the coping stones

Big Merinos, Subway & KFC

Big Merinos, Subway & KFC
Neo-colonial kernels scatter their seeds
that sprout neon & concrete over Australian Dreams
Sub-terra root systems tunnel underground
Enlightenment darkens First Nations sight

Time silenced scarred trees uproot for fast food
Rootless tubers desiccate a cracked earth
Saline soils weep willows, replace natives
with red-necked vegetation bush-tucker erased
Across on Gundungurra massacre fields
Fizzy Reds hurl tornadoes in Union & League

Merino ramifications fleece stewards
Graziers squat on forgotten, land, Captain
No Beard skull & cross bone Union Jack-in-the-boxes
cross off dictation *tests*
Officers rear their sunburnt Country heads

A red & yellow Shell shock serrates
like tussocks, Paterson's purple curses
blow-in, turn the air blue with pollution
To my left a giant red hammer awaits
another nail in indigenous hollow logs
Multinationals provide fossilised fuel

Utes guzzle, strapped to their sides in tools
Fill up with fried chicken at Red Rooster
e & G pea green, blue line underneath

Urged by fresh food people to save 4 Cents
                Ampol's red domino leg leans forward
as market momentum accelerates
Eureka flags & Southern Crosses fly
behind white picket ringfences alight
Jack & Jill sit on their verandahs & rock
Sheltered settlers under bullnose rooves
Display homes for frontier attitude

Prados with chrome bull bars steer capacious
car parks, barracking Raiders & Eels number plates
On the lookout for Roos with attitude
New house rules on auction blocked TV screen
reality, how other, half-caste are removed

Snake Path

An early summer springs
Sunlight extends its fingertips
& stipples eucalypt shade
in zebra stripe brilliance
I see flies hovering a-buzz
of activity, then realise
    the orange brown elongated belly
                                                  skin hatching like eggs
                                                              stretches my surprise
                                                                      brown snake laying on my path

Cobain's Plaid Pain

Myths out of matter, matter out of myths

Matter out of myths,
myths out of matter
Kurt's tattered flannel
plaid out in fragmented ceramics
loose threads piece them together

Blue tartan collars rock in Seattle
& lumberjack Washington State
Flannel shirts, torn jeans
Draught excluded through sleet, snow
the mud & rain

Courtney gives clothes to the Goodwill
in thrift stores the love & pain
Randoms now walk the walk,
masquerade as Kurt Cobain
Rock stars materialise fabric memory
anti-fashioned nirvana
catapults souls into stardom & fame

Freewheel (Kaleen to the City)

I freewheel down Northbourne in a dawn daydream
along Ellenborough's fallopian tube
connecting model suburbs, Lyneham to Kaleen
Past the sleepy complex peace of The Sanctuary
near where gym junkies HI(I)T an early Next Gen fix
through cow parsley pastures making memories
Soon skies develop duplexes into high-rise Dickson sights
that deliver me to a teeming Mouat Street

I freewheel with eco warriors behind me
Civvy fatigues enlivened by lycra,
Briefcases morph into pannier saddlebags
Follow the pleats of APS officers and Gen Z
tadpoles and grey nomads breathe
as we escape into concrete green canopy
Now its public housing chic, Crispin's dingoes
bark past the scarred trees & tent embassy

At each traffic light I recapture breath
Spring air cleansed, my denim jacket protects
Right chino leg tucked into business sock,
In time with the metronome of my cobalt tie
pendulum, then I remember Dad on his fragile
racing bike, leaving at 7.30, regular as spokes turning
his life & mine in parallel trajectory wheeling free

Perdure

Taino & Arawak tightens local cheekbones
Akwaaba ricochets a Black Atlantic Cape Coast
to Suriname, Akropong to Accompong
Marooned nouns kept in abstract aspic
Timeless gel embalms the memory
Braithwaite's creole landscape reverberates
Steel pan Atlantis glint
Join Walcott's dots in Omeros
as fishermen heave salted dreams

Leura

There's a world out there beyond your windowsill
Under Leura blossoms, a Hellenic-Aussie talks
Of Athenian mores, unearthing stories like horses from husband Troy
how her family mined gold
Olden day stories where coins lay on eyelids
& Charon rows

At the Sparrow nest into an egg & bacon brioche,
Avoid the sepia tourist signs that boast waterfalls
Cascade the Blue eucalypt haze down

To the mid mountains where Lawson
Tucks itself into a corner, as far as it can from the roar
of Sydney bound metallic cans, rest at Lyttleton Store

& enjoy its cooperative wares
The doorbell rings, a latch clicks into distant place
Where there exists stillness in bygone airs

The aspidistra keeps flying defiant
foxgloves suckle nectar honeysweet reminiscing
The church crenelations outline the front cover

like a Ladybird book, trucks belch to Western suburbs
You avoid it all as you sit on the kerb

Master Jalebi

Master Jalebi sits in his Wigram
Street weatherboard cottage
His sons slow traffic to a jam
with the Master's amber jalebi
In amber neon summer heat
we venture in, walls adorned
with passport stamps from Karachi
to Harris Park & order tikka masala
Kashmiri naan spreads its
desiccated diaspora, we tear
coconut & red peppers
before we dive into the spices

Cotswold Stone Heart

Etched in my memory—Deddington
red sandstone gateway to the Cotswolds
Far from his Goulburn home

I think of Knowlman on tour
Turning his racing wheel
the other side of the world

rebuilding an edifice brick by brick
& I think, trapped in aspic nostalgia
Of my first mini trips, after earning my licence,

how sandstone turned into flint
at the forgetting of my eyelid
near Bristol borders, how Bibury yellow

turned autumnal at Netherswell Manor
Stowed on the wold, swotting for A levels
Perplexed by untamed shrews

who eschewed my advances, swatting me
like one of Donne's metaphysical fleas

SalUSbury WORLD

A Londis black plastic bag of pistachios
Gifted, a present from an Iraqi *dad*
Super sweet Somali tea in a thermos
In a safe spot pod, calmed by carda*mom*
Salusbury World, down from the bridge
at Brondesbury, dreidels spin נ nun, ג gimel, ה hei, ש shin
while cinnamon doughnuts encrust hungry lips
Grandpa Goodman sits stoically for Year 3
& quips in the tempo of the lively
about how his red & white yarmulke
is an Old & New Testament to survival

S & M

In a post Britpop blur
Damon & Suzy chill
Long since beetlebum tin
foiled ships sunk
They're in love, Damon orders
iconic sausage & mash
whistled between the ivories
Part Colchester drawl
Crowned in flat cap ironic Mockney
words slur post pub crawl
The next best thing to jellied eels
But this is the West not East
where occidental eccentrics
who once knew Leyton
orient themselves for pleasure
whilst LPs spin in Leisure
Trussed uncomfortably
in chained leather
Under the gaze given celebrity

A Star Flattery

Mum flatters as a form of resistance
Quick akwaaba charm
Trolley half full of bargain granny smiths
She barters Leighton for Makola market
Sun smacked Ashanti, coast golden delicious
Comfort flexes in Beds, Fanti, Twi & Ga
Lately she's Leighton indigenous
Hyperlocal vocal attraction star

Unfurl

Palm unfurl choked by sticky weeds
The curvature of a snail shell
anachronistic anemone,
three thousand leagues under the sea
Drexciyan survivors breathe
Fast forward from the pregnant pause
From hollow doors return Afrofuture progeny

At Harris Park

Dusk is hungry for night
Stars bumper to bumper at Harris Park,
Sikh stickers twinkle & dangle Tiranga
Saffron strong, moon's white peace looms
in Dharmachakra overtures
Lotus floating inner peace
Law's wheel unmoved in the pond
In verdant sea spread diaspora seeds

White Khanda on black flag signals Langar
My imagination irrigates
dry hunger with naan, roti, chapatis
A man proffers jalebi on a tray
Tangerine neon separates night from day
Deep fried pretzels dipped in sugar syrup
I wipe my lips in Harris Park anticipation

Bin Truck

Post Pilates, a mum crouches lycra-clad
Her lad is strapped & cushioned in a pram

She points towards the jaws
Household waste tipped out in haste
Black liners pulled like chewing gum

A dad wheels the red one,
His adolescent son grabs the yellow lidded bin

To trigger reminiscence
How he carried him

To watch the garbage emptying
'It's hard to think

how this lad was once in a pram.'

Charted

I've charted these paths, the viaduct
mist hung like Saturn's rings, linen dirty
Dunny lane wrung, Olympic symbols rust overlaps
A worm twitch on fresh bitumen
Snails stipple their escape trails

while Aboriginals to Country cling
Our glistening stitches of confluence
Barricade us false in confidence
River crossings by sun sizzled pilgrims
peregrinate Goulburn's Great South Road

Fitzroy's timber replaced by iron bridge
Strong against rainbow snaking floods
Of foreigners, Marulan stone piers fear
the croak of Chinese blokes in frog's hollow
Mining seamlessly for alluvial gold

William Punch's trip: Gallipoli to Rocky Hill
Hidden histories seldom told
Left unsaid, midden dead on rubbish tips
Like flimsy timber in storm crumbling
A wicker basket jail made in rubble

Prisoners stroll off until the next
is bricked, so soft convict spoons out dig
Huff and puff can't blow their houses down
Fortress Australia settled by convict ships
sailing super-maxxed perimeters

The African Look

Rainbow attachments for different grades
Frank's clippers fade while Auntie's wrists weave-on

Brazzaville Afrobeats play out their song
lines like cornrows dream Kinshasa Bills

Ethereal as gorillas in our mi(d)st
Auntie asks if Frank needs a new cross-over bag

She can get her hands on all the brands
Frank buzzes my 'fro like a mosquito on heat

A *star* squashed into an aste*risk*
One minute innocent, next boy soldiering

'Which is the branch that interprets the law?'
Auntie quizzes her friend on citizenship

Eyebrows knit upwards on furrowed brows
'Is it the judiciary or executive?'

She's right, practice for new age dictation tests
Her friends laugh with joy, 100%

Hybrid Mishmash

For Peter Burke

'All cultures are the result of a mishmash'—Claude Levi-Strauss

Ahenema slip into a Nike Vortex, box
a portal, Imran's shalwar kameez,
kufi capped with '95 Air Max
Yinka's batik messages billow with bottle
Hoist the broadsheet, 5th plinth Nelson's Column
Thai saunas, Zen Jews, Nigerian Kung Fu
Big Ben Zephaniah's British melting po(e)t
strikes to stir primordial soup
Encounter, contact, interact, exchange
Make mishmash on the rarest grooves
Mix n' match it's all the same

Riots of Colour/ Time Bombs

I

As 'them' seek Brexit from Empire's stage
Brixton riots curve into shielded vitrines
Transport me forward-back to '81
into a black n' white zeitgeist ticking time machine
Throwback   molotov bombs
                              sweep Wood Green to Woolwich
Handsworth, Chapeltown, Moss Side,
Incite, intoxicate toxic Toxteth
Stop n' search for answers in monochrome
Rasta tams spin their kaleidoscopes
          To divine Zion, Home
Fryer's riot of colour, have staying power

II

Iron Lady's fist smashes Scargill
Brassed Off minors inject coal seam veins
with Steely Dan's needles to numb pain
Punk rock new wave do the two tone reggae
Reach inner and outta cities
Ghost towns deep in recession Tory torn blue
Ska, rocksteady ready for Handsworth v2 revolution

Once Upon My Time

Once upon my time, I write
myself, two exclusive histories
My story into one unity
One kintsugi kente tako-tsubo pot
of the broken, found & lost
The return to roots
comes to term with routes
Multiple, a youth sutures into story
like Cuffay & Daley tailoring, stitches
each wound, each bruise, each confusion
into a beautiful journey
Rainbow contusions
Paths of distinction, figuring
Every road a finger triggering

Phrases From Dad

Skinheads on rafts (baked beans in the '80s)
More grease to the elbow (keep on going)
Canteen medals (you've dropped food on your top)

Phrases on the Wall

Keep Britain White
Wogs Out
This is NF Territory
Stiff Little Fingers
Free (Patrice) Lumumba
Pakis Outnumbered 10 to 1

Hybrid Heaven

I'm worn up, wound into a fashion
watching ACF & Nicholas stitching
Africa, Caribbean & Europe, together
We enter hybrid heaven

I wear a Léopoldville Bill stetson & bolo
doff my trilby to tailor gods
Juteopolis hopscotch Scotland
to Jamrock, Angola to Mexico
Tartan Rasta tams
crisscrossed with police helmet blocks
across Panama, Dreads tucked in
Galápagos baker boy hats, together
We enter hybrid heaven

I see Boyd's canvas
with stippled revolutionary glue
Pirates' eyes patched
to distort the view
Numb skull & cross bones on Union Jack
Xanthorrhoea Black boys out fox botany
Baying natives replace Emmanuel, together
We enter hybrid heaven

I tune into Hannah's poem
listen to Lowe's rhythms flow
Ilford, China & Jamaica
organised like passengers
On a yellow, brown & black star liner

in iambic pentameter, together
We enter hybrid heaven
I hear Kamau, once Edward
renunciate his consonants & vowels
tap out at a Southbank lectern
the skim of a pebble
across Saltponds to Labadi
The Departed & The Arrivants, together
We enter hybrid heaven

I underline Gilroy's theories
scrawled notes in multiple margins
In the heavy lead of 2B pencil sharp
Until I become blunt, knowing
postcolonial melancholia
& convivial culture kings
Manuscripts inked by multicultural monks
scribe on Hall's palimpsest
to test my identity
Beyond Tebbit's lilywhite cricket tests
& Thatcherite tick box citizenship, together
We enter hybrid heaven

Morning O(we)d(e)

Good morning lovely
Is it morning or night
Dusk or dawn?
You are for me
Life's bookends beyond the shelf
My living breathing dream
Yours are the sheets
(sweet in musical cliche)
without an accent
I want to be between

Jamrock-Juteopolis

Nicholas knits Jamrock-Juteopolis
Greenwich meantime, Cuffay master tailors
kintsugi kente from varnished sugar cane fields
stretching from Chatham, then Tasmania
Gilroy shifts convivial culture
& post-war melancholia, over a Black Atlantic
Dreads together in inclement weathering

A grass turf mohican sits
On Churchill's skull, bring down the plinth
Colston topples in trip-hopping Bristol
Yinka's fifth column ship in a bottle
sits on Nelson's Column, navigate the margins
Billow our batik souls, all adrift
Until we find our Zion, Jamrock- Juteopolis

Wexted Warm Up

8.42am, Wexted Oval, Goulburn

I

Formed like fencers with foils
Oxley College boys
lick the seams of red apples
Scrump & pluck
Two lads in parallel paddle bats
into the ether, they straighten
Wire muzzled gladiators
in hard hats

II

The bowler runs up to windmill deliveries
Lily arms sail Southern Tablelands spring sea
Batsman grist for the white willow mill
Behind a picket fence boundary
Stumped by a system, jailed without bail
Gentlemen's games declared piracy

Walk the Plank, Tread the Boards

For Jason Allen-Paisant

Othello walks through
The marbled city;
his skin betrays him

He is striving against
Badmind. This is Othello's life -

I walk the plank torture
The country town fortune
or fate?

Eyes fixed, I dial down
the blackness
Wearing my blazer, chinos
& tie (noose-like I despise them)

Eyes fixed in defiance
I & I is the survivor
in this inhospitable **Island**
nation of mongrels

Who forget, they're leaky
Boat People
who mumble & whisper
How did I arrive?

The lady looks in the pram
Blonde hair, whisps of golden curl

& those cerulean eyes
Cherub from heaven
She fixes me like a kidnapper

I walk through the bubble
& chatter of Salamanca
Save the Tassie diablo plushies
blush, the rush for rediscovery
The thylacine -
But where are the *aborigines*?

Transported in Cuffay's DNA
this is tailor made history
Kente stitched across oceans
Doors of No Return
Middle Passages beyond   bondage

The moor walks
Through deepest darkest Beds
Herts & Bucks, Stockgrove Park
Ashridge, Ivinghoe Beacon
In 'Progressive Counties'

heads spin like windmills
More grist for resilience
The tide of blue rinses
The grimaces

The pen oozes its black bruised
purple ink pain
between the lines
Of the physical & psychic
open space

Embodied, constructed, occupied
by otherworldly controversies
International-Domestic
Hyper-glocal

I'm a hemisphere half left
& whole again
Transblacklantic-Afropean

I play
like Cuffay & Daley
Stitching up
Kintsugi kente keloid scars
in hardened liquid spill

Eritrean Taxi

Uber #3

The Uber smoothly moves, hovering
Chic electric along Federation [2]
Iceberg drifting on bitumen

Flinders Station sparkles its gold rush
hour in the city of immigrants

At Federation, alight the hidden history
Our Eritrean driver recalls
A Civil War, Band Aid propaganda

then families spread in the West-
turn into subaltern suburbs

Wyndham, Brimbank, Hume, Melton
Moonee Valley, Yarra, Maribyrnong, Casey
Seeds floating bitumen seas
Taxiing the earthly skies too long

ICA4US

For Dean Cross

In the window of an iPhone lens, reflect
On Modern Gods, the tractor heads
homage to neolithic figures monochrome
hewn out of mettle, Easter Island stone
The number gold plates the burning dream
ICA4US
all is not what it seems

Trucks tear along the Hume, flying too close to blaze
I'm driven too close to the core's furnace

1:1 with a ten-tonne truck
the wedge-tail eagle hovers above
My face elongates bull bar stainless steel,
arms heavy, leaden, with waxy feathers stuck
I follow the image as it shrinks to grow

Hit by a mirage life's flash dims
Bright, parallel to my country town
The rush of wind pressures diamond-like
tin thin, it shakes me, the wobble within

Road-train-metallic-camel-caravan
carries trauma on Atlas' shoulders that span
continents forged by commodities

MACK flies the flag of das KAPITAL, in breeze
No beard pirates spear Union Jacks

banners banish aboriginals
in terror nullifying traps
mega fawning retreat to the Anthropocene

The tinted windscreen wraps around
tradies' sunnies obfuscate the landscape shroud
in black and white shadowing hate
dull pindan, spinifex, corrugations
Petrol guzzling heads choke 400 nations

As we head long in the dust clouds
to an Emerald City on an ochre brick road
Leave peroxide fields for synthetic turfed homes
& laterite paths pave iron awe & gold

We breathe in pollutant mutant fumes
in opium dens masses consumed
Road trains, load our carriage of freight
linked like slaves on a supply chain
to supermarket storage facilities

The rosary bead preaches its genesis
Find Zion, EXIT, Exodus
Leave country towns for big smoke at all costs
The weatherboard splinters, fibros collapse
A neon glimmer pulls, attracts

MACK carves its tread on colonial tracks
rut large in the pindan clay sand
like the forearms of a junkie, black,
veins bruised, beat & blue blood
Inventions cave in a smartphone frame pinch

Black & white pathos stretches canvases
in pigment print, processed by 'victims'
Front to back the tractor head shrinks
Depths of colonial corridors cleansed,
inverting the photoshop in grey scale

Yet at the precipice, edge of a cliff
Hit by a truck, I fall like coyote
Wily, I look around then pause
Neo in the matrix pulls Anansi's bungee strings,
bouncing back to absorb shock & grow wings

At the chasm, we survive cataclysm
Between brushed steel sentinel exhaust stacks
Bunjil hovers on the wind deflecting

In his dream rig memorial, a shape shifts
I make out dad's outline beyond the windshield tint
Daedalus honks his horn at me then waves!

The wedgie soars over the number plate
ICA4US, symbol of status & fate

Obsessive Compulsive Order

At 10
Scuffed fake DMs, rubber rattles my sole
I cross the Scout Hut at Hockliffe Road
Fleur-de-lis in racing green, points north
I open my Puma holdall to check...
... if my lunchbox is still there

At 30, 40...
Oxblood DMs shine cherry red
I close the door & turn the knob
right, left, right
Count to ten, repeat again
Obsessive compulsive order of thoughts

Ordinal & cardinal syntax holds me back
at the front door, fear the trespass
The open wound invasion
The bloody handshakes clot my mind
Drip through each membrane

As I pore over impossibilities
Permeate each synapse
I wish I could forget, relax

Anonymous Haiku Interlude

poetic vocation
Owen careers into
protean portfolios

dishwasher
down & out, Paris, London
doleful

band of cotton sea
beyond the shadowed
eucalypt ridges

the creak of a thousand
doors to heaven
cockatoo chorus

Ben's Back in Africa

Ben's Back in Africa
The DRC to be exact
Accounts on his technicolour showreel
Fly posted all over his Instagram
Oscar told me, he was scrollin'
Thirteen years since he's seen his dad

I taught him for a term, when he was in Year 5
Before I fled the rednecks for Canberra
Lent him a picture book about the Congo
Gorillas in the mist, an opportunity
The images persist
Hoping, I'd foster a connection
Generate happier recollections

Recently I've seen him parking parallel
to the Wexted entrance, in a silver sedan
Adult chiselled face & rope twists
Trips to the gym ripp(l)ing late teen muscle
Crepuscular time doesn't stand for the young
In middle age I discover it sprints
Larrikin still, he drives past his twin sisters
Benita & Beninya, twice half siblings
Ben stops then revs past them & laughs
before he yanks the handbrake of a guffaw

Over the years our paths have crossed
I've seen him around Merino County
Bois d'ébène debonair

sleek in black shirt hospitality
serving drinks to blue rinses at the Workers
Wolves in goats' clothing
In the equator of the equation, I calculate
if Ben will ever become Egide again?

Self
Love

The counsellor says,
I've got to love myself
So, I hug him at three
a toddler wearing a Goofy
T-shirt (designed by Disney)
Side-parted nappy afro,
Knee high
red & white hooped socks
& sky-blue shorts
Lost & found far from home

The counsellor says,
I've got to love myself
So I cuddle him
at six(es) and seven(s)
as the playground beckons
Growing harder
Sticks & stones calcify
to burnt toast & nig-nog nigger
bounty bar & oreo

The counsellor says,
I've got to love myself
So I sit side by side
With him at eleven
as he flips the pages
of athletes, he points

In favour of each black man
that's faster on the track
Parallel with each contorted
torso on each bend
The baton passes
From Jesse to Carl & Ed

The counsellor says,
I've got to love myself
So I'm wide-eyed when
Mum discovers *Comfort Herself*
I reach for Brother Malcolm
off the shelf
then feel the Steel Pulse
Of a Handsworth Revolution
from my cosy bedroom

The counsellor says,
I've got to love myself
So I snuggle up close & listen
To him in adolescent vigour
Pent up angst, sardonic cynicism
as he shouts at his mum
soapy slap bubbles numb the throb
his red raw jaw
Why don't we belong?

The counsellor says,
I've got to love myself
So I lie down next to him
at sixteen, hearing Marley
From afar, I & I

Is a Lion of Judah

The counsellor says,
I've got to love myself
I press play & he records
Hit the North
on sellotaped cassette
Madchester raves
To Stone Roses & Happy Mondays

The counsellor says,
I've got to love myself
So I console him at eighteen
When Zion thwarts
& calls him obroni
When he reaches Kotoka
& realises so many blacks
He's never seen
Wo ho te sɛn? The only fragment
Left
Of the tongue he flexed in Baby Twi
Bereft of vowels & consonants

Fixed

Feet fixed by Bundy rum, at Flamingos discover
Goulburn's red neck underbelly
Rich & smooth brown sugar doesn't soothe
These wounds, wound up & down
By this myopic country town
Where we're welcomed like snakes serrated in tussocks
Cursed like Paterson's Aborigines & Lebs
Still the regions don't vote YES

They tousle my afro & ask
Which part of South Africa am I from
Part of a dark continent who see half
rather than the double in front of them

I long to be back in a Kilburn kaleidoscope
Where continuum hues flow—
Beige, golden brown handshakes, fists bump in khaki shades,
Bring back & forth from fifties ignorance
Masonic lodges in an apron tied headlock
Icy CWA rooms festooned with homemade cakes
Fake smiles & uncomfortable handshakes

Raw & Wild

I

On Bong Bong Street, it's raw & wild
Street sides sprout mugwort, ashwagandha for camomiles
In mid-30s spring heat, shades coconut tea
Leaves you fresh, shelter, replenish in the reign
Of plant powder smoothie criminals
Who'll rob you of your Aussie dollar
Pill-grims nutri-bullet proofed excuses
for prices high as the mercury rises

We gurgle in gentrified elixir, worshipping
Our bodily temples rub sandalwood incense
Mantras chant our new Saint Steviol
Monk fruits extract confessions with glycosides
Genuflect to the modern gods raw & wild

II

Hashtag new hybrids, plant powered by biofuel
Who breathe in the oil seed rape of the masses
Produce slaves bound to gut friendly lifestyles
We align our chakras & bow our heads,
enhance our chances, by
Amino-acid-probiotic branch-chain-gangs
Amen

We digest our own MCT enzymes
Medium-chain-triglycerides
Lean muscle ripples & recovers while hiding
stomach banded bot-tox lip(o)-suction

Punters bow to read labels feverishly
Ayurvedic medicine at the right price
Feel energetic, inspired, alive
Trust me, it’s vegan certified.

Out of Love

I fell in love with the green and sandstone
Cathedrals cobbling it together
I'd met Heather from Braddy in NW Territory

I fell in love with freestanding housed lebensraum
where I couldn't tell a semi-de(b)t from a terrace
Spring from summer or autumn weather

Now I'm out of love with the country
Like a leaf plucked from a toxic tree
The blonde brick veneer has let me down

Desperate now to leave this town
Down & out of love, cobbling it together

Trappers

Whilst I drive my mind passes by
A joey pup baking in Southern Tablelands sun
Kangaroo meat seals the road I travel on

By Collector Creek commuters applaud
choices for the spoilt, on temptation's hoardings
SOME CAFE claps its Monopoly letters

Spelling cryptic messages from Charlotte's Web
Like Anansi's span, super tensile
Heatherbrae sausage rolls, a golden M tempts

I glance the flash of Fed Ex trucks nestled
at Baxter Road, then I see a Trapper
dressed in Rabbitoh green & red

Bunging on his billy tin of myths
Two score n' ten back, Keith & Bill were trapped
rabbits in the Bannister bush, filthy with self-pity

As dusk hushes itself, Bill lights the camping fire
To ignite damper from a swagman,
bought several years before

The essential ingredient of a bush tucker story
Now the bakery s(w)erves commuters to Sydney
Industrial camp ovens shine in glory

Wolves in Merino Clothing

Wolves in Merino Clothing
Drenched against blow(n)-in foes
They bleat they're the first
Far from anchor fresh off the boat
Superfine stereotypes
brand us & them apart
Wool pulled over eyes & classed
at stores, after the saleyard

Inland City

At the CCTV gantry, hover
Fox head pylons connect us to the grid
In the matrix, we're urged
To reduce speed & turn left
Exercise caution in blue eucalypt mist
Enter the rising bitumen if you dare
A sepia sign declares it's heritage welcome
To the historic first inland city
Of lilac, thirsty roses & prejudice
Whether Jew, Chinese or Indigenous
Aboriginals hung out to dry in crime
like dirty linen left on racks inside

Strange orange fruit
in Guantanamo baying costumes
Super maxxed by red necked rusty screws
in correctional service uniform
Wolves in Merino clothing
In Surveillance Capital Country
an abattoir of artifice flexes indus-
trial muscle, its rib cage incarcerates
as genetic memory falters under lie detection
Natives in DNA corroding chains
On the precipice of Rocky hillbilly recollection
Welcome to the first inland city

Kangaroo Bones

Kangaroo bones puncture tyres on the road
Landscapes burn under the cloud burst
OF HEAVY STEREOTYPES
A leg cocks in rigor mortis starfish position
as you try to look aside from its posterior eye

The fresher ones lay foetal
One hundred and fifty million years ago
We shared an ancestor
Twenty thousand shared genes

Noxious weeds prick the nature strips
Fox bait paves yet to be graded bush escapes
How many dead bodies does Lake George hold?
I forge travel flashbacks
to Como's salmon art nouveau
Mirages under mountains marbled in snow
To powerboats carving Coniston Water
Electric metal pebbles skimming boats
Kangaroo bones line my Remembrance Driveway

Nightclub Sirens

In deep tunnel vision I dug with moles
I wobbled with them in their drinking holes
Leg bent flamingos with bar side appetites
to the depths of destruction numb they bite
& sink bar-be-queued shrimps shocking sunburnt pink
Crabs & hot gossiping lobsters stick
From Frog's Hollow to Bundy carpets fast

With middle-aged women I danced around
their handbags at the nightclub dawn to dusk
Diamante studs cluster like magnet rust
Eyes wide saucers, sorcerer magic attracts
Venus' fake lashes up & down flap
to catch the eye of lost boys bombed by love-
bitten by lust's loss, Dutch courage viscous
twice thicker than blood orange victims, sucked
Dreg legs slide slowly down the hourglass
Amber aspic tumblers decant a last
chance, aleatory roll of the glass, whiskey

Chasers meet Karens, Sharons, Sashays & Kims
Unironic post-Cobain saviours sin
Lads flounder in flannel, jeans (af)fray R(.)I(.)P
Pain killed to enter nirvana bloodstream
by ice pipe, opiate & cannabis gateways
plaid out in chequered patterns of dysfunction
Karma stamped letters of introduction
FACS, CSA & AVO truncheons

bludgeon us in nouveau culture customs
Mums shriek, 'How ya goin', fancy a drink?'
Botox lips syncing in the bubble slur-ry
The flotsam & jetsam of promises
UDL elixir fills their ruddy
Cheek by jowls at the Belmore fountain trough
Treading bitter, botanical waters
luxuriant lemon-lime green torture

Amidst the disco fog & dry ice strobe
Sons & daughters lost, a long way from hope/ home
The Ngorongoro Crater evaporates
Cinderellas catch taxis before it's too late
Mascara crosshatches on Blombos rock caves
Once this was civilisation's cradle!
'til Captain No Beards erased coolamon graves
Sound the klaxons to ghostly strangers rave
Open ears & eyes to silent nightclub sirens

Hibiscus Defiant

for David Oluwale

Hands cupped, Yinka sucks hibiscus nectar
in the clouds that creak open from above
optimism dripping from his sun kissed lips

Shango conducts kintsugi kente lightning
in a perfect orchestra of thunderous applause
Soon Oluwale's blue plaques precipitate the cityscape

dousing the flames of racial hate
In its place at the South Bank, morning glory sprouts
supplant to supersede our tears without a doubt

that run to hide from copper coloured crime
Risen from River Aire despairing, we breathe
diaspora stars of David, defiantly

Hibiscus filaments flower to enlighten everywhere
Sta(y)men & women powerfully charge
Growth's hope breaks bondage, burgeon ten metres high

Bright leaves offer umbrella shelter
for children dressed in batik finery
In our roaring forties sails raise to catch, trade winds

from the Indonesian Far East to Europe,
Nigeria, Benin & Ghana by *handelaar*
Death bears next season's fruit
          to reap a future seeded in peace & opport**unity**

Cool as f**k

This guy, you'll agree, is cool as f**k,
he hovers, a Zeppelin without the lead
Zephyr on Vespa, a breath of fresh air
Lambretta revving, yet Stephen's flown
on an inspiral carpet ride from home
across the Bass on a hydro-tre-foil

to treble our luck, his Uber arrives
against G-force odds, hovers chevrons, glides
along Sutton's upper echelons mobile
Where ponies foxtrot on hobby farms,
picket fences extend showjumping poles
& commuters recharge electric cars
for clean green trips to the ACT

Servants catalytically convert
the public eye them suspiciously
While they vie for top positions
amidst solar-panelled valleys that heat dreams
Under greenhouse gases the masses fume
IT crowds cloud nimbus acronyms
APS officers salute, bow heads
graded 1 to 6 in deference,
9 to 5 time stamps rank & MS Office file

EL1s & 2s at sixes and seven
figure salaries balance fat cats
on their knees & sip Veuve in cliques
Alphas & epsilons lick Rizla+ sheets

to the wind, catch the last of the roaring
forties, before it's too late mate
On the chaise longue class Bs untie tongues
merrily exchange tales of when they raved
all night long
                    & came down
                                        from capital vowels with bongs
Stephen's travelled from Burnley to TAS
in a post-breakdance windmill spin
Like Windy Miller from Camberwick Green
Escaping Calder & Brun Lea cotton mills
post-industrial revolution ferris wheels

chasing paper streams in dragons' wake,
at the Cuvier & Derwent confluence
Deep in fashionable Tassie
Thanks to a microdot com boom,
proved wise in-vestments
Embarrassed, he's indebted to luck
Jazzy B-boy in his Superstars, parallel

Three Dassler black go faster stripe
beneath his jacket a Breakfast Club T-
shirt quotes, *We Are All Bizarre It Seems*
Head to shell-toe drip, dressed in cobalt suit sheen
Limp Platinum hair hangs undercut
Pulled by gravity & wax, defying cheeks rise
into a smile, behind graphic designer specs,
the corner of his mouth lifts, wrinkles crease eyes

In Burnley brogue, accented by Lancs
we talk of flat caps, woolybacks,

Yorkshire tea, cricket & Mancs,
wars of the roses & those notorious
indie boys who were made of stone,
waiting to be adored, happier
Mondays, bygone Madchester zeitgeists,
bowl cut sliced bitter lemon regret
wash down waterfalls, we resurrect
terry towelling bucket hats & Joe Bloggs jeans
Bellbottoms aloft on inspiral carpet
rides to Aladdin's cave at a palace, Afflecks
& Eastern Bloc classifieds

We spend bubble gum memories at Sally's
vending machine, old skool sweet dreams
Rumble fish out of current stream
floundering and tortured poms
Milltown Brothers who are cousins
Recollections revolve, stuck in vinyl groove

We enter 808 States to MC Tunes,
re-take a trip with Northside to strawberry fields
Freaky Dancing with 24-hour party
people who carnt smile 'cos the white out
Squirrels and G-Men weave the Free Trade Hall
Wrote for Luck, lyrics scrunch behind Shaun's back
betwixt raised curtains Moet swig

Now close to our mid-centuries, hold back
the bat, step off the crease,
in case of pills, thrills & bellyaches
at halcyon Hacienda days, we eschew
a joint after a four pack, maybe just two

of whitey declining wisdom, yesteryear flashback

Stephen's smile & mine widen in time
with the first bar of a fool's gold wah-wah
Pedal reveries along a yellow brick road
Digitally remastered maracas implode
pyrite dynamite crystallises home
Shake percussive antipodean hope

Windellama Bus

On the Windellama bus, Southern Comfort
Bundled into rucksacks while vapes suck
under school jumpers, welcome to Bus 11
Where kids run & jump onto KTM heaven
Revving their (pre) pubescent engines
Headlong on ungraded roads, bumpkins
In apple, spud & pumpkin country
Where Bundy rum lines pool & rumpus
rooms infused with rough & tumble

One Four All

One Four shanks, shivs to split citizenship
Elocution drills in Multicultural English
Chicago to Kennington, Harlem Spartans
reach Rooty Hill, braggadocio myths
Replaced on walls sprayed with street lyrics
Of forgotten horrors in satellite cities

Bars challenge too many Cook's narratives
Ploy postcode wars broth stir 21 districts
Technicolour dials tune up monochrome
Mounty bops ride high ponies

Beats challenge Home & Away Australia
Turf wars supplant surf shacks, drill & rap
Fibro eshays outplay silvertails
Vanquish St. George, dragon slayers
Hip hop, rap & drill saviours
One Four's chorus ricochets radio waves
Western subs machine gun their arsenal

Yet YP Celly & Lekks get incarcerated
for a message, against all odds
Pub drawl slackjaw assaults White Australia
claims lay indignation at 'foreigners'

In a Jurrasic Park of mega flora fauna
Join One Four all's multicultural chorus
Above the roar of strike force raptors
who enact terrorist nullius martial laws

Like Anansi we'll weave & avoid capture
Pulling the silky strings of our larynxes
Exo-skeleton phalanx plantation tactics
Little fish swim, minnows against apartheids
Lyrics spit worldwide three million streams
Incendiary messages with bottle, can't be silences
Survive & master crimes of violence
Reaction videos worldwide webs ripple digital echoes
Backed by Streatham Dave, Kamilaroi kids
that refigure the edifice of colonial ghettoes

All Pasifika put fingers on swastika triggers
Niggers with attitude, Netflix without chill

4x4 Warriors

Four by four warriors haul Jayco caravans
Over Gundungurra land daubed totem turtle wax
Albatross neckties compete to look flash
Number plates stamped with nomads' tales
gate between blue Victoria's Place to Be
Marooned by views of Queensland Sunshine State
In the exhaust fumes expel four hundred nations

Swags attach themselves to roof racks
Marin mountain bikes sway their pendulums
Toyota, Tiguan, VW Tooraks
as we travel the Hume Highway forth & back
Petrol, electric & hybrid engines
Raptors snarl a Great Dividing Range with menace
rev two & four door dual cab injections

Inoculate, vaccinate vacations in dream place(bo)
Tree changers divine sea, reverse country escape
Tyres tread slalom chevrons & white dashed lines
Double demerits read on amber dots
Revenue raises travellers with fines
Breathe in speeding targets for RBTs

In policed holidays seasoned drivers
Cross New South Wales & ACT borders
Jayco caravans hauled by four by fours

Chinaman's Beach

White mist sky above the boardwalk
Moves its watery grains in time
To a planet woven into hour glasses
My canvas is for now a seascape
The gentle wrinkle of the morning wave
The easy highway roar
of moon pulled tidal wake
The ebb & flowing froth on crushed coral
bubble & flip flop thong squeak
Mysteries on porcelain Hyams beach
Through Jurrasic Jervis to Chinaman
We funnel through a colonial jungle
            Where once sailors, pirates
                        & Yuin discovered

E-Whiplash

For my nephew Henry

My nephew Henry listens to the e-whip
lash of plantation narratives, he will not crack
Though cyberbullies push buttons in the clouds
thick as bittersweet molasses from cut cane
bleeds resilient pain, strong in broken places
          kintsugi kente lines the frag-
                    ments of a broken calabash

Tik tok sends e-messages down our spines
one generation at a time
Shallow ringtones that bring it all back home
half a millennia and still counting on an aba*cus*
Our beads of exasperation bleed dry

Where are Mansa Musa's salt and gold caravans?
We, the camels of history
who store up truth like a baobab tree
who thirst for epistemology, pick the leaves
fruitfully forbidden we seize
Massa's crop to shatter glass ceilings

Pilgrims on Walcott's Adamic mission
all, doubly conscious of du Bois vision
aboard Omeros odysseys, follow the sea swift
Slaveships capsize for Garvey's Black Star Liners
that navigate the world of space and time
We harvest, whilst sickle's scythe sweeps Europe
In Ages Dark, its cauldron bubbling

with bubonic pus, the troubles of infected rats
Whilst we grew mosques and libraries
Griots picked our histories on kora strings
Look through rose glass windows, alabaster frames

Yet in the high school corridors of Leicestershire
Still, Henry hears tik tok time capsules drop
electronically detonate race hate bombs
Soon, we will explode these shells of ignorance
white fragility across Black Atlantic seas,
With molotovs, Afropeans: Black Russians,
                    Afro-Saxons, pied noir
                         Diaspora's seeds blossom from afar

Only so many times, can you headlock,
wrestle and punch them out to break the deadlock?
Anger unfurls and flashes its dreadlocks from tams
I and I, Zion traveller, a Rastaman
Enlightenment bright like Shango's hammer
heritage's message home to drown out the ringtones

Afrofuturists look back on Igbo landings
on planet Earth, Al-kebulan disturbed
Anvil on a gavel, the time is now

We will continue to sing our songs
through innocence and injury, we live
twice thick kintsugi keloid scars that heal
We turn our heads 360 degrees, in courage
Back and forward, shrug off the whiplash

Genesis

It's New Year's Eve 2023
We see a genesis of a new movement on TV
Screened, red mohican & Cuban heeled
Double-breast silk tassel Icarus sleeves
Fans scream while Owusu shoots nutri-bullets
blending genres out of stayed grooves
To the consternation of aspic Australia
Sydney Harbour ripples a punk rap new wave
From Koforidua's womb to Canberra cradle
Owusu rolls a stone from a tomb

Afterword

Planetary Bio(me)

I'm a two-tone Ska suedehead, former dread Marley rocksteady revivalist, an indie shoe-gazing kid participant observing anthropologist revising limited narratives, Maangamizi non-apologist, a missile heat-seeking reparations yesterday for post-traumatic slavery syndrome hanging in limbo Anansi. I'm an unapologetic haibun hybrid-syncretic lyrical individual part of collective genetic memory, prose poet cup twice full, magic mulatto, every ready Duracell, Brer Rabbit plantation tactician shattering shackles, shapeshifting Anansi spanning Ghana, Japan, the UK and Australia in short circuitry. A transformer escaping torture, para-normally moved by Kamau's tidalectics, pulled by Asase Yaa's Jupiter moon, Dogon saucer high-flyer on a Starship Black Liner steered by Garvey, wearing Yinka's obsidian helmets in batik spacesuits verse-a-tile tessellating in the polysemic tailoring of William Cuffay and Nicholas Daley, clad in ACF all-weather, all-planet Blackpacker Gypsy spacefit worn by Afropean Afronauts like Johny Pitts, stitched with invisible Don Letts safety pin pulled grenades, bobbing like exotic Black Russian molotovs, from Hannibal to Pushkin. I'm an Afrofuturist searching AI adinkra algorithms to replace radiating raciology with infra-red planetary humanism. African Intelligence. I'm a Drexciyan Survivor, Harlem Renaissance Man breaking down pseudo-scientific ladders of evolution, Nyankopoxyican Revolutionist floating in a Sautiverse.

About the Author

Andrew is an Anglo-Akan-Australian writer and educator teaching across secondary and tertiary settings, including Creative Writing and Cultures and Diversity at the University of Canberra. His work explores liminality, identity, and the social constructions of race across transnational spaces. Having lived in the UK, Japan, and Australia, his writing interrogates belonging and cultural hybridity.

Author of the novella *Nicked Names* (2022), Andrew's poetry has been widely published in journals and major anthologies, including *The Best New British and Irish Poets 2019–2021*, *Poetry for the Planet*, and *Nombono*. A recipient of two Best of the Net Awards, with nominations for both the Pushcart Prize and the Rhysling Award, the work reflects an ongoing engagement with transnational identity and form.

Poetry collections include *Japanabandon, Manifest.oh!, Diaspora³, Objections, Scars & Artefacts* (2023), and *Outside of Here Outsider Hear!* (2024). Andrew's eighth book, *Childish Recollections,* is forthcoming with Black Spring Press Group.

www.ingramcontent.com/pod-product-compliance
Ingram Content Group Australia Pty Ltd
76 Discovery Rd, Dandenong South VIC 3175, AU
AUHW020611080726
429626AU00003B/6

9 781764 106894